The treble (and sopranino) recorder

Holding your recorder

Left hand at the top,
close all the round holes,
use the cushions of the fingers
(not the tips).
Left thumb closes the back hole,
right thumb supports the recorder.

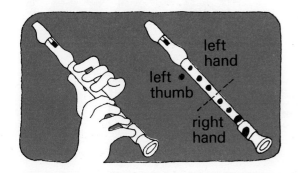

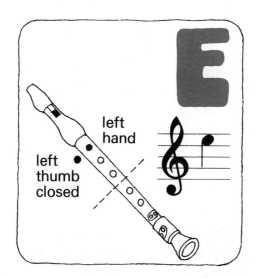

To play E

Lift open all the fingers
except the top finger and
thumb (left hand).
Breathe the note,
don't blow hard.
Tongue the rhythm
with tuh or duh.

1

Slow tune

The King's drummers

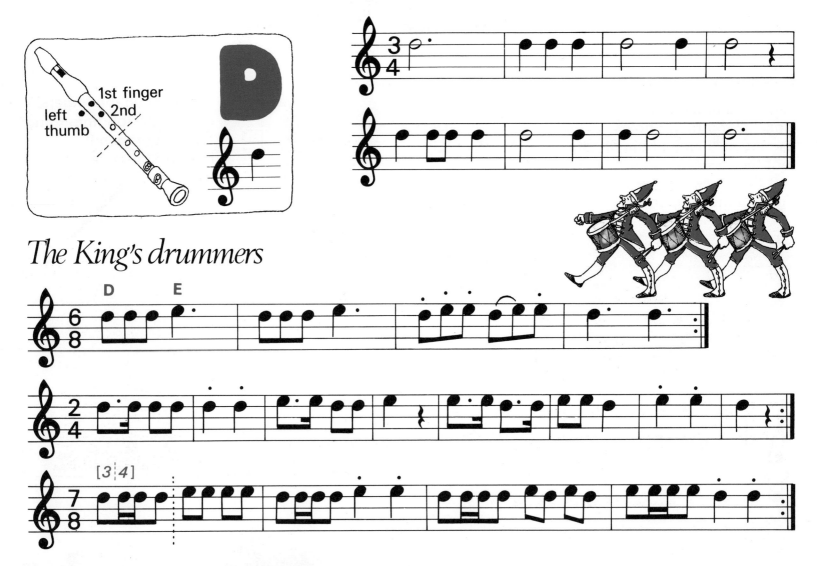

Horses

D E

John Smith fellow fine, can you shoe this horse of mine?

Old farmer Giles he rode se-ven miles.

This is the way the ladies ride.

A farmer went trotting u-pon his grey mare.

Ride away, ride away, Johnny shall ride.

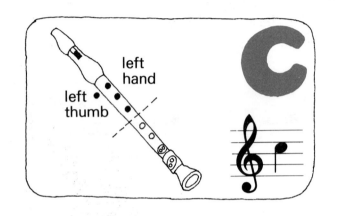

Counting out

Ibble obble black bobble OUT goes SHE ——.

One po - ta - to,   two po - ta - to,

Quickly

Playground

Margo Fagan

Smoothly

Swinging

Quickly

Rhythmically

Ballooning

Slow and floating

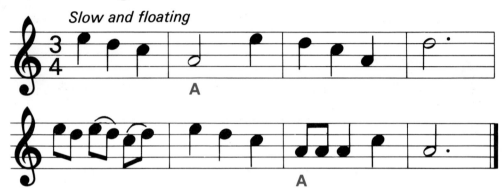

A

Gliding

Smoothly

C   D   E   Margo Fagan

A

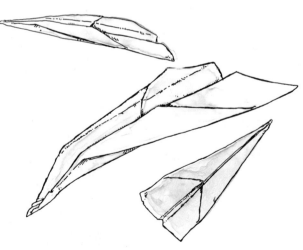

Trains

At a steady pace

Margo Fagan

Getting quicker and quicker

As fast as you can

Getting slower and slower

Bells

Old Dan Tucker

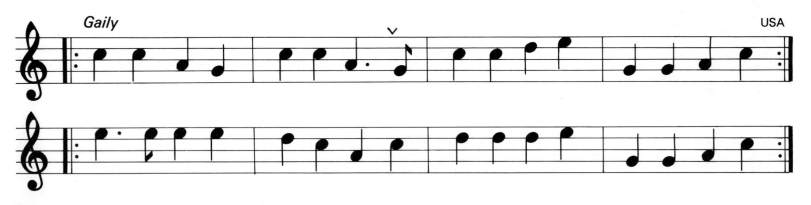

Gaily

USA

Fishing

Margo Fagan

Rather slowly and smoothly

When I was a little boy

USA

Brightly

Old Macdonald

Brightly

Traditional

Strathspey

Slowly

Margo Fagan

Bought me a cat

USA

Puppet show

Lilting

Margo Fagan

The new building

Hammering

Margo Fagan

Painting

Sawing

Now it's yours !

Put in the win-dows, paint all the doors, fit up the cur - tains, polish the floors.

Climbing

Street game

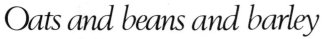

Oats and beans and barley

14

Au clair de la lune

Moderate speed

France

Georgia's tune

Flowing

Oh, Susannah

Happily

I saw three ships

Gently

England

Nonesuch

Quick but flowing

Playford 1650

Fine

Da Capo al Fine

London Bridge

Briskly   Traditional

Stands a lady

Simply   Traditional

The rakish highland man

Scotland

Highland fling

Margo Fagan

19

Kum ba yah

Rather solemnly

Africa

Leave her, Johnnie

Steadily

England

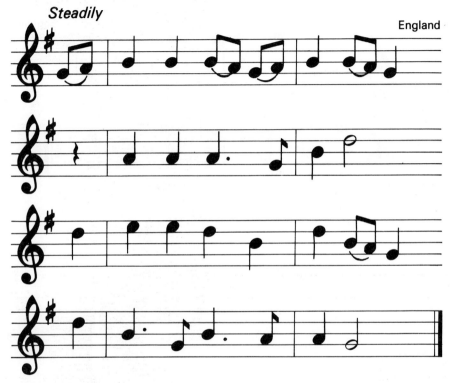

Lavender's blue

Smoothly

England

21

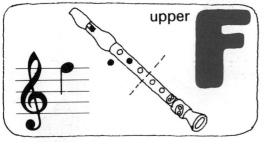

upper **F**

A soul, a soul, a soul cake

England

Mocking bird

Sweetly   **F**   USA

Yankee Doodle

Gaily   USA

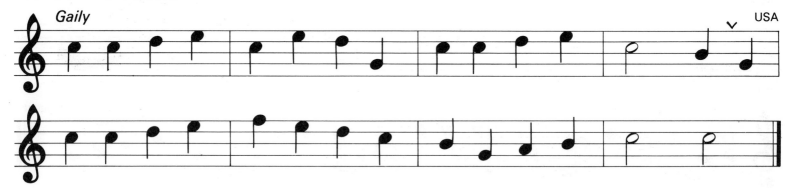

The `Navvies´

Bright and rhythmic

Country dance

Steadily

France

24

Moors and Mountain

Flowing

Margo Fagan

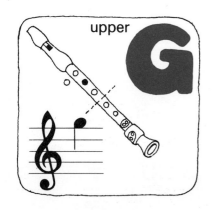

upper **G**

The streets of Laredo

Sadly

USA

Down in Demerara

Brightly   Traditional

Grandpa's snuff box

Jolly   France

Daisy, Daisy

With a swing

England

Row, row, row your boat (A round)

The cuckoo (A round)

Girls and boys come out to play

Happily

England

Fine

Da Capo al Fine

Tomorrow shall be my dancing day

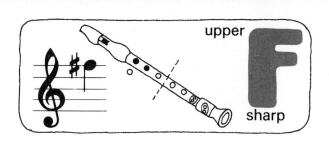

upper **F** sharp

The farmer

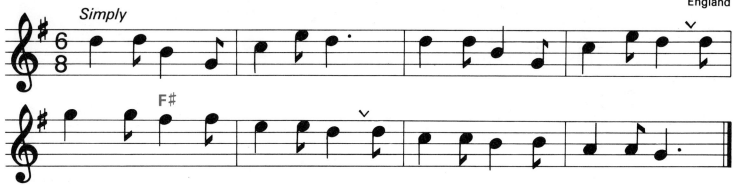

England

Simply

F#

Cornish dance

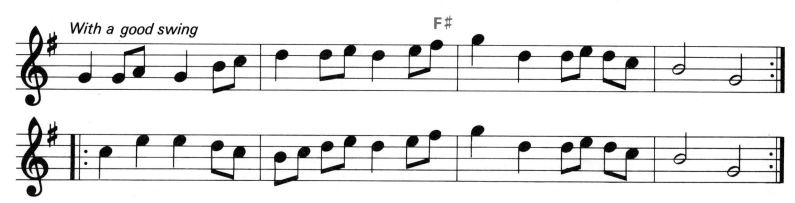

With a good swing

F#

Koymenayo

Jolly

Liverpool

Morris dance

Fast F#

England

33

Barbara Allen

Rather sadly

Traditional

Lullaby

Peacefully

Russia

When the swan sings (A round)

England

Ebb tide

Margo Fagan

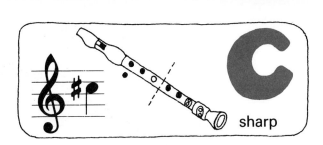

sharp

Jingle bells

Brightly

USA

Singing game

Quite quickly

France

36

Gretel's song

Simply F#   C#   Germany

The bluebells of Scotland

Oberek

38

The parting

1776 England

With a swing

Fine

Da Capo al Fine

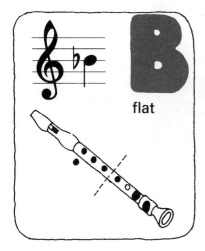

flat

Ah, poor bird (A round)

England

Canoes

Smoothly

Margo Fagan

40

A-working on the railway

1841 Ireland

With a good swing

the
lowest
note

Twinkle twinkle little star

Not too fast

Fine

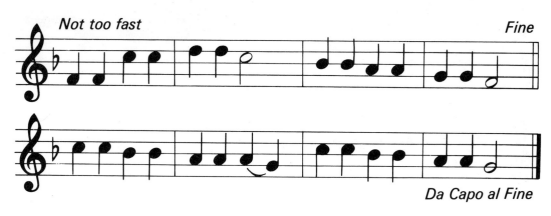

Da Capo al Fine

Trumpets

B♭ **Bright and rhythmic**

Margo Fagan

F

Il était une bergère - The shepherdess

Simply

The wood in evening

Gently

Margo Fagan

43

Goodnight ladies

England

Steadily

Eb

Brightly

44

The quest

Simply

England

Rose, rose (A round)

Smoothly

England

O how lovely is the evening (A round)

England

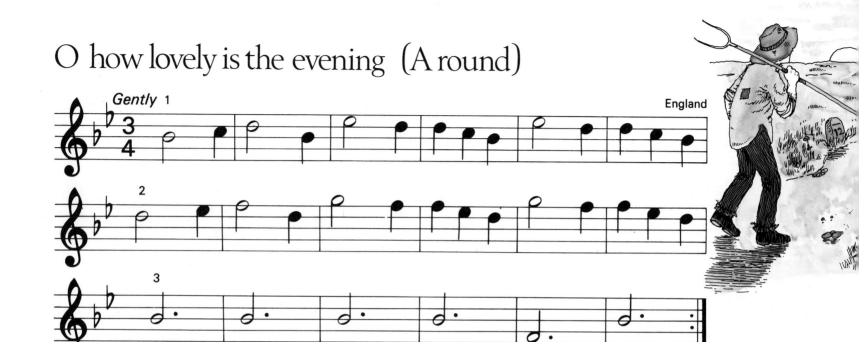

Thistle and heather

Margo Fagan

Ye banks and braes of Bonny Doon

Flowing

Scotland

D sharp sounds the same as **E** flat and has the same fingering.

Dancing game

Rhythmically

Poland

C♮